Reading Essentials
in Science

DOWN TO EARTH!

Soil Science

TRACI STECKEL PEDERSEN

PERFECTION LEARNING®

Editorial Director: Susan C. Thies
Editor: Mary L. Bush
Design Director: Randy Messer
Book Design: Lori Gould, Michelle Glass
Cover Design: Michael A. Aspengren

A special thanks to the following for their scientific review of the book:
Jason Parkin; Meteorologist; KCCI Weather; Des Moines, IA
Jeffrey Bush; Field Engineer; Vessco, Inc.

Image Credits:
© Bob Rowan; Progressive Image/CORBIS: p. 16 (right)

Photos.com: front and back covers, pp. 5, 8, 9, 10, 11, 12, 13, 14, 15, 16 (left), 19, 20, 24; Corel: p. 7 (left);
© CORBIS/Royalty-Free: p. 4; Photodisc: all background images, all sidebar images, all chapter numbers,
p. 7 (right); Sue Cornelison: p. 6; Perfection Learning Corporation: all paper bag backgrounds

For information, contact
Perfection Learning® Corporation
1000 North Second Avenue, P.O. Box 500
Logan, Iowa 51546-0500.
Phone: 1-800-831-4190
Fax: 1-800-543-2745
perfectionlearning.com

1 2 3 4 5 6 PP 10 09 08 07 06 05

Paperback ISBN 0-7891-6609-7
Reinforced Library Binding ISBN 0-7569-4633-6

Table of Contents

1 Just Dirt?

Most people avoid dirt. We're always washing it off our hands, spraying it off our cars, and sweeping it off our floors. Dirt is muddy, messy, and just plain "dirty."

Actually, though, dirt is a very important part of life. But when we talk about dirt in a good way, it usually goes by another name—soil. Dirt and soil are really the same thing, but the two names seem to have different meanings attached to them. For example, when you plant flowers in *soil*, you get *dirt* under your fingernails. What's the difference? Nothing, except

that the soil you plant in is good for your flowers and the soil under your fingers is "bad." Dirt is just soil with a bad rap!

Depending on Dirt

Whether you call it soil or dirt, you depend on it every day. In fact, all life depends on soil. Soil is home to many types of animals such as groundhogs, earthworms, insects, and millions of tiny **organisms**. Soil is also necessary for plant life. It holds the water and **minerals** that plants need to grow.

Plants play an important role in the life cycle. Plants release oxygen into the air for animals to breathe. They also provide food for many animals, including humans. Even those animals that eat only meat rely on plants. That's because many of these animals eat other animals that *are* plant-eaters. For example, lions are meat-eaters that feast on antelopes, which are plant-eaters.

Soil also helps control and filter water. Can you imagine how much rain would run along the ground after a storm if there were no soil to soak it up? Flooding would be a huge problem. Luckily, soil provides a solution. It absorbs most rainwater. Then it uses the water to nourish plants or passes it on to other bodies of water or storage areas for human use.

So the next time you think it's just dirt, think again!

A Look at the Layers

The Earth consists of several layers. The inner layers are made of hot rock and metal. The outer layer, or crust, is made of rocks and soil.

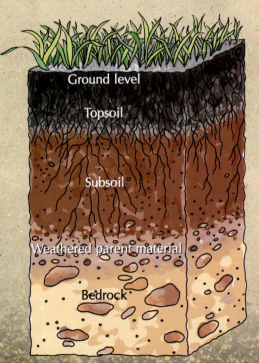

The crust has layers too. They're known as **horizons**. **Bedrock**, **weathered** parent material, **subsoil**, **topsoil**, and ground level are horizons in the Earth's crust.

Bedrock

The bottom horizon is solid rock called *bedrock*. Most of the Earth's bedrock is well covered by upper layers of rock and soil. In a few places, however, the bedrock is exposed at the surface. This is called an *outcropping*.

Weathered Parent Material

In the soil family, the rocks are considered the parents. That's because soil is "born" from pieces of rocks. Above the bedrock lies a layer of these broken rock pieces. These pieces came from big chunks of rock that were weathered, or broken down, by wind or water.

Subsoil

The subsoil is a mixture of rock particles and a small amount of **organic matter**. Organic matter is material from living things. Much of it comes from the remains of plants or animals after they die. In soil, this organic matter is called **humus**.

The subsoil holds much of the soil's available minerals and water. Deep plant roots seek this layer looking for the **nutrients** they need.

Rock outcropping

Ground Level

On top of it all is the ground level layer. Plants and animals live on the ground level. People walk, live, and build on it. This layer is rich in organic matter. It is often covered with dead leaves and other living things that will soon **decompose** and return to the soil.

Topsoil

Topsoil sits on top of the subsoil. This layer contains a large amount of humus. It is perfect for sprouting seeds and growing roots. Many creepy-crawly creatures wriggle through the topsoil, mixing up the humus with fresh air. This helps the material break down even further.

The Scoop on Soil Formation

Bedrock is solid rock. Topsoil is loose, crumbly soil. How does bedrock eventually become part of the topsoil? It's a long process that is influenced by the rocks involved; the climate; plant and animal activity; land features; and time.

A Rocky Beginning

Soil begins with rocks. As rocks are weathered by wind and water, they break into smaller pieces. These pieces mix with other materials to become soil. The rock pieces provide the minerals that plants and animals need for growth.

Bedrock

flows into the cracks in rocks. When temperatures drop, the water freezes and splits the rocks apart.

As the weathering of rocks occurs, a small amount of soil is born. At this point, however, the soil is unable to support most plant life. It doesn't contain enough of the rich organic matter that plants need.

The type of rock affects what type of soil is formed. For instance, a bedrock of sandstone will produce a sandy soil.

The Weather Forecast

The climate in an area plays a major role in the weathering of rocks. The climate is the usual weather in an area. Wind, rain, and ice are weather forces that break down rocks. Temperatures also affect weathering. For example, when temperatures are warm, water

Breaking It Down and Building It Up

As rock and soil are broken down into smaller pieces, they become home to numerous organisms. When these organisms die and break down, they become part of the soil. The minerals from the rocks and the nutrients from the organic matter make the soil a better place for plant life. Soon plants sprout and thrive. When these plants die, they add more organic matter to the soil. As the cycle continues, the soil becomes more **fertile** and is able to support more life.

Soil Likes Lichens

Lichens (LEYE kuhns) can grow without soil. These organisms often make their home on rocks instead. While they grow, lichens secrete acids that wear away the rocks. Eventually this creates new soil material.

Decomposers are soil's best friends. Decomposers help plants and animals become broken down into nutrients that other plants and animals need. Fungi such as mushrooms and many types of bacteria are decomposers.

You may think of earthworms as yucky things that you use to catch fish. But earthworms are actually important decomposers. These wiggly creatures eat plant and animal material as well as bits of soil and rock. They digest this material and then get rid of waste in the form of **casts**. These nutrient-rich casts make the soil more fertile.

Earthworms also "stir up" the soil as they burrow through it. This mixes air in with the soil. The oxygen and nitrogen in air are necessary for decomposition. The more air available, the faster decomposition occurs.

Soil Formation

It all begins with rock.

The rock is weathered.

Decomposers do their part.

Fertile soil is formed.

Feature Factors

The land features in an area can influence soil formation. Mountains, for instance, make a big difference in an area's soil. Since water flows downhill, the soil on the top and sides of a mountain absorbs much less water than the soil at the bottom. Soil higher on a mountain is also more likely to be carried down the mountainside instead of building up in deep layers. On the other hand, soil deposited at the base of mountains is likely to be deep and fertile.

Water traveling across land can also affect soil. Rivers that flow across an area pick up and drop off rocks and minerals along their way. This makes the soil along riverbanks very fertile.

Only Time Will Tell

Rocks break down and mix with organic material to form soil. It may sound like a simple process, but it's definitely not a quick one. It can take hundreds or thousands of years for the soil in an area to reach a mature point where it's healthy and stable. In a mature area of soil, new soil replaces soil that is washed or carried away. Fresh humus replaces the humus used by organisms. All of this takes time, but it's worth it.

4 Sorting Soils

All soils are formed in the same basic way. However, soils come from different types of rocks and minerals. They can have particles of different sizes. Soils can also have different **textures**. Soils are classified according to these unique characteristics.

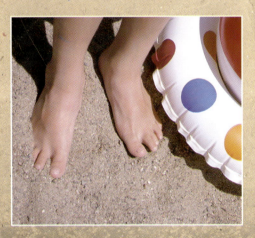

Sand

The main mineral in sand is quartz. Quartz doesn't weather very easily, so it has larger particles than other soils. Picture the size of sand grains at the beach.

Sand's large particle size means that there are bigger spaces between the particles. This gives sand a loose feel. It will run right through your fingers when it's dry. If you've ever made a sand castle, you know that you have to mix sand with water to get your castle to "stick" together.

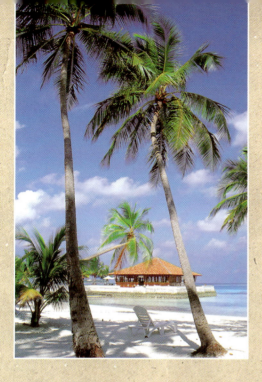

tongue. To compare particle sizes, imagine that sand particles are about the size of a dime. Silt particles would then be about the size of the period at the end of this sentence.

Silt *is* able to hold water and nutrients that plants need. This makes it good for farming. However, because it is so light, silt is easily carried away by water or wind. Silt is often found in floodplains, the areas around rivers where minerals are left behind by flooding.

Because of its "looseness," sand isn't able to hold water or nutrients well. This makes it unsuitable for growing crops. Some plants with deep roots, however, are able to survive in sand. These plants can reach the subsoil to get nutrients and water.

Silt

Silt is finer and stickier than sand. Grains of silt feel smooth when touched but gritty on the

Silt

Clay

Clay

Clay particles are very tiny. If silt were the size of a period, then clay particles would be too small to see without a microscope. There is very little space between these tiny particles.

Dry grains of clay feel smooth. However, when the grains get wet, the clay feels sticky.

Plant roots have a hard time pushing through clay. Organisms are unable to breathe in the tight spaces. So pure clay soil isn't good for growing. However, having some clay in soil is important because it absorbs harmful acids and provides valuable minerals.

Loam

All gardeners and farmers want the perfect soil. This type of soil is known as loam. Loam generally has equal amounts of sand and silt as well as a small portion of clay. This soil recipe creates just the right amount of space between particles. Air and water can pass through, but nutrients don't leak out. Plant roots can spread out. Humus can build up. Loam is a grower's dream come true!

Comparing loam (left) and sandy soil (right)

Inquire and Investigate: How Much Water Can Different Soils Hold?

Question: How much water do different soils hold?

Answer the question: I think that different soils hold_____.

Form a hypothesis: Different soils hold (different/the same) amounts of water.

Test the hypothesis:

Materials

- 4 one-gallon plastic milk jugs
- scissors
- ice pick or other sharp-tipped tool
- 5 cups each of sand, silt, clay, and loam soil
- permanent marker
- liquid measuring cup
- water
- watering can
- 2 aluminum pans

Procedure

- Cut the top off each milk jug. Ask an adult to help you punch a lot of small holes in the bottom of each jug. Make the same number of holes in each jug.
- Fill each jug about half full with one type of soil. Label each jug with the soil type.
- Measure 1 cup of water into the watering can. Hold a jug of soil over a pan. Sprinkle all of the water over the jug. Observe what happens. Measure any water that drains into the pan. Record all of your observations.
- Dump out any water in the pan. Repeat the process with each type of soil. Compare your results.

Observations: The sand will hold the least amount of water. The silt and loam will hold some of the water and allow some to pass through. The clay will hold the most water.

Conclusions: Different soils hold different amounts of water. Sandy soils have large spaces between their particles, so water passes through quickly. Clay soils have small spaces, so water is trapped. Silt and loam soils have medium-sized spaces, so they hold enough water for plant life while allowing excess water to pass through.

chapter 5

The Science of Soil

What makes soil healthy? How can we control soil **erosion**? How can we improve soil so crops can grow better?

Pedologists are scientists who study soil. They work hard to find the answers to these and many other questions about soil.

Scientist of Significance

George Nelson Coffey is considered the first American pedologist. Coffey joined the Bureau of Soils in 1900. During his time with the bureau, he studied soils all over the United States. He realized that soils could be classified according to their common characteristics. Coffey spent many years mapping soil and studying soil erosion.

At first, Coffey's ideas about soil were mostly ignored. Years later, however, his work was rediscovered by other pedologists. They realized that Coffey's ideas about classifying soils were correct. This method of sorting soils is still used today.

Keeping It in the Ground

Erosion is a serious soil problem. Erosion happens when soil is moved from one location to another by wind or water. For example, wind can blow away the topsoil on a farmer's field. Flooding can wash away the fertile soil along a river. In the United States, soil is eroding almost 20 times faster than it's forming. More than half of this erosion is due to human actions such as poor farming methods, **deforestation**, and the overgrazing of cattle.

Scientists have studied soil erosion and offered solutions to the problem. Planting trees and other plants in open areas helps soil stay put. The roots of plants anchor soil in the ground. Trees block winds from sweeping soil away. Building windbreaks also helps keep wind from reaching open patches of soil. Grazing lands should be rotated so all of the plant cover in a field isn't removed. Farming practices can be improved to prevent the erosion of farmland soils.

Smart Farming

Good soil for growing crops is actually hard to find. Imagine the Earth is an apple. If you cut that apple into ten pieces, about one of those pieces would represent the area on Earth with fertile soil. If you peel the skin off that piece of apple, that's how much soil is available to produce all of the world's food supply.

In natural soils, plants are allowed to decay and replenish the soil with nutrients. In farming, however, the crops are pulled out and the soil loses its nutrient source. So how can farmers produce crops and still keep the soil healthy?

No-till field

Soil scientists continue to find better ways to farm crops. One solution is to add fertilizer to poor soil. Fertilizers are organic matter and human-made chemicals that increase a soil's ability to grow plants.

Fertilizer in garden soil

Another method is no-till farming. Traditionally, farmers tilled, or turned over, their soil when planting seeds. This disturbed the soil and released some of the minerals into the air. In no-till farming, farmers plant without turning over the soil. This helps soil keep its rich layer of humus and prevents erosion.

Growing crops is an old profession, but even farmers can benefit from new technology. Today, many farmers use precision farming technology. This approach uses technology to gather, store, and analyze information about the soil in a farmer's fields. A single field can contain soil with different characteristics. By knowing which areas in a field are best for which types of crops, farmers can make better decisions about their planting.

The equipment in precision farming can locate different soil types in a field and map out the information for a farmer. It can also keep track of how much of a crop certain soils can produce. Some machines can even control how much water and fertilizer are delivered to a field. It's a whole new way of farming—one that makes the best of the soil a farmer has.

Crop rotation is also a good farming practice. Instead of planting the same crop over and over on the same field, crops are rotated from year to year. This helps keep the soil balanced because some crops take certain nutrients from the soil while others replace nutrients. Crop rotation also helps reduce erosion since some crops hold soil in the ground better than others.

Planting cover crops is another proven farming method. Cover crops are protective plants that are grown to improve the condition of the soil that main crops are planted in. Cover crops help control topsoil erosion. They also replace nutrients used by the crops.

Soil Solutions

Soil is necessary for life, and in turn, life is necessary for soil. Studying the soil and using this knowledge to take care of it will benefit everyone. So the next time you get dirty, stop and say thanks to the soil that supports you!

Internet Connections and Related Reading for Soil

http://school.discovery.com/schooladventures/soil/soil_safari.html
Take a soil safari, get the dirt (facts) on soil, and meet some of the creepy-crawly creatures that make their home in the ground.

http://www.soil-net.com/schools/
Get schooled on soil—what it is, where it's found, and how it's important.

http://yucky.kids.discovery.com/flash/worm/index.html
This "yucky" site will introduce you to earthworms and their job as "recyclers."

http://www.fieldmuseum.org/ua/default.htm
Go on this interactive underground adventure to discover the amazing world of soil and the animals that live there.

http://www.enchantedlearning.com/geology/soil/
Dig into dirt with this information on soil types, formation, and horizons. Print out a label-your-own-layers sheet.

http://www.nrcs.usda.gov/feature/education/squirm/skQstns.html
Worming your way through these questions and answers about soil will make you soil smart!

* * * * * * * * * * * * * * * *

Dirt: The Scoop on Soil by Natalie M. Rosinsky. Discusses the nature, uses, and importance of soil and the many forms of life that it supports. Picture Window Books, 2003. ISBN 1-4048-0012-3.
[IL K–4] (3429606 HB)

•IL = Interest Level
Perfection Learning's catalog number is included for your ordering convenience.
HB indicates hardback.

Glossary

bedrock (BED rahk) solid layer of rock

cast (kast) solid waste material from a worm

decompose (dee kuhm POHZ) to break down into smaller parts; rot

decomposer (dee kuhm POHZ er) organism that helps break down other organisms (see separate entry for *organism*)

deforestation (dee for uh STAY shuhn) removal of a large number of trees from an area

erosion (uh ROH zhuhn) movement of soil by wind or water

fertile (FER tuhl) good for growing; rich in nutrients (see separate entry for *nutrient*)

horizon (hor EYE zuhn) layer of rock or soil

humus (HYOU muhs) rich part of soil that is formed from organic matter (see separate entry for *organic matter*)

mineral (MIN er uhl) nonliving substance found in rocks and soil that plants and animals need to live

nutrient (NOO tree ent) material that plants and animals need to live and grow

organic matter (or GAN ik MAT er) remains of organisms (see separate entry for *organism*)

organism (OR guh niz uhm) living thing

subsoil (SUHB soyl) layer of soil that's a mixture of rock particles and organic matter (see separate entry for *organic matter*)

texture (TEKS cher) how something feels, especially how rough or smooth it is

topsoil (TAHP soyl) upper layer of soil that's rich in nutrients (see separate entry for *nutrient*)

weathered (WETH erd) broken down into smaller pieces by weather forces (wind and water)

windbreak (WIND brayk) wall or other barrier built to block or slow down winds

Index